2ND EDITION

PIANO

Adventures®

by Nancy and Randall Faber
with Victoria McArthur

THE BASIC PIANO METHOD

This book belongs to: _____

Note: All exercises and pieces are by
Nancy and Randall Faber unless otherwise noted.

FABER
PIANO ADVENTURES®

3042 Creek Drive
Ann Arbor, Michigan 48108

TECHNIQUE SECRETS

These four Technique Secrets are used as daily warm-ups for pieces and exercises in this book.
The "secrets" may be learned gradually and are highlighted in gold-colored boxes throughout the pages.
For quick and easy use, the Lesson Book also refers to each correlating Technique Book page with this icon: ✍

The teacher should demonstrate each "technique secret" as it is introduced.

Four Technique Secrets

Technique means skill. These technique secrets will help you play pieces more easily.

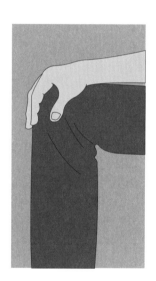

1. **The first secret is ROUND HAND SHAPE.**

Hand Cups

- Place your **right hand** over your kneecap.

- Keep that "hand shape" and s-l-o-w-l-y place
  your hand on the keyboard.

- Now do the same with your **left hand**.
  Try it hands together!

2. **The second secret is a RELAXED WRIST.**

Wrist Float-off (on the closed piano lid)

- Set your hands in a rounded hand position.

- Pretend a balloon on a string is slowly pulling your wrist
  upward. Let your wrist rise in s-l-o-w motion until only the
  tip of finger 3 is touching the surface.*

- Now gently return to a normal playing position.

- **Do 2 "wrist float-offs" with right hand, then left hand.**
  Try it hands together!

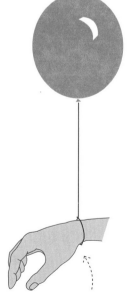

*Teacher Note: The shoulder should not rise, but stay relaxed.

📖 Lesson p.8 (Firefly), p.10 (Little River)   FF10

Teacher Note: The next secret teaches staccato, allowing the hand to bounce lightly from the wrist. The student should be coached to relax while tapping, so as not to stiffen the forearm.

3. The third secret is a LIGHT HAND BOUNCE.

Woodpecker Taps (on the closed piano lid)

- Place your **R.H.** in a rounded hand position.

- Perch your thumb on the *side tip* so your wrist doesn't sag.

- **Lightly tap this rhythm with your R.H. fingertips.**
  (all fingers tap together).

R.H. Tap - ping, tap - ping   on   the   tree,

- Repeat *Woodpecker Taps* with your left hand. Now tap hands together.

4. The fourth secret is FINGER INDEPENDENCE.

Finger Talk (on the closed piano lid)

- Silently play the **finger pattern** below. Remember to keep a round hand position.

- Play **right hand**.

- Play **left hand**.

- Play **hands together**.

1 - 2 - 3 - 4 - 5 - 3 - 1
└──── finger pattern ────┘

Legato means a smooth and connected sound, with no break between tones. When you play LEGATO, one finger goes down as the other finger comes up.

Technique Secret: **round hand shape**

Warm-up with *Hand Cups* (p. 2).

Sticky Fingers
Legato Steps for R.H.

Butterscotch Fingers (Remember to play on the *side tip* of the thumb.)

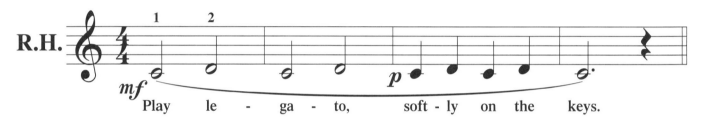

Cotton Candy Fingers

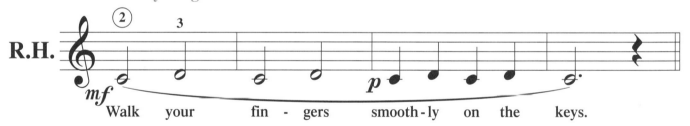

Caramel Fingers

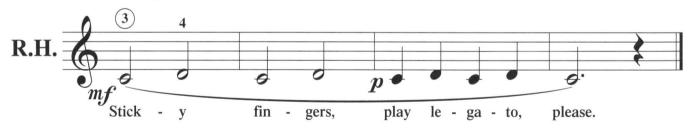

Teacher Duet: (Student plays *as written***)** Use this duet for both pages 4-5.

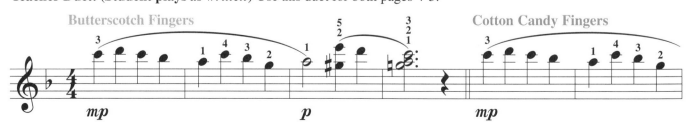

4   Lesson p.10 (Little River)   FF1097

- Which of these ideas remind you of *legato*? (circle two) ✏

popping corn   a flowing stream   a bumpy road   a rolling ball

Sticky Fingers

Legato Steps for L.H.

Butterscotch Fingers (Remember to play on the *side tip* of the thumb.)

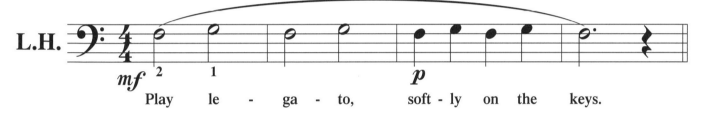

Play le - ga - to, soft - ly on the keys.

Cotton Candy Fingers

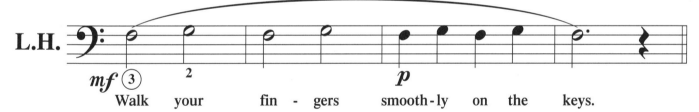

Walk your fin - gers smooth-ly on the keys.

Caramel Fingers

Stick - y fin - gers, play le - ga - to, please.

Caramel Fingers

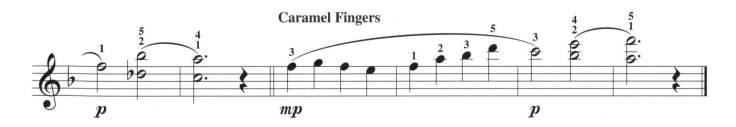

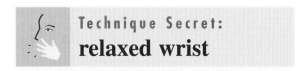

Technique Secret:
relaxed wrist

Warm-up with *Wrist Float-off* (p. 2).

Smooth Take-off
(for R.H. alone)

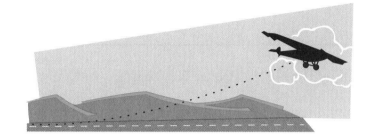

This exercise uses a **SKIPPING PATTERN**, repeated higher up the keys.

• Technique Hint: Lift gently from your wrist
at the end of each line.

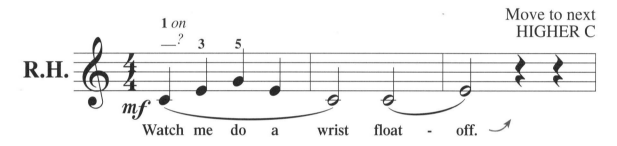

Watch me do a wrist float - off.

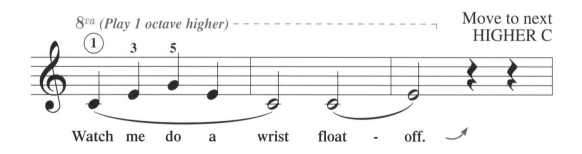

Watch me do a wrist float - off.

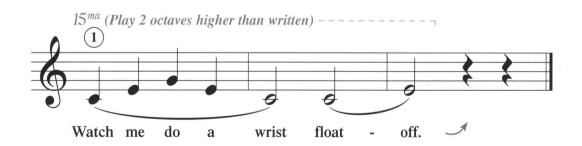

Watch me do a wrist float - off.

Memorize this musical pattern and play *Smooth Take-off* by memory.
Watch your "wrist float-offs" as you play.

Technique Secret:
relaxed wrist

Warm-up with *Wrist Float-off* (p. 2).

Smooth Take-off
(for L.H. alone)

This exercise uses a **SKIPPING PATTERN** for the left hand. Listen for a smooth legato.

- Does your wrist float off on the *first* or *last* note of the pattern?

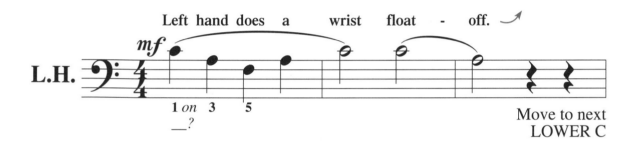

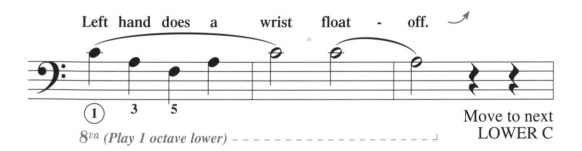

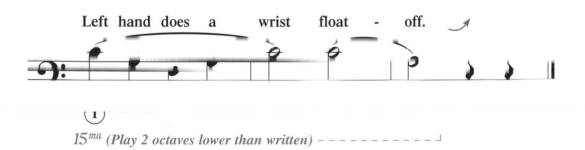

- To imagine a "wrist float-off," picture a gentle wind lifting the wrist up,
  then setting the hand down again.

Staccato means the notes are separated to create a crisp, bouncy sound.
To play staccato, lightly bounce from the wrist. Stay close to the keys!

Technique Secret:
light hand bounce

Warm-up with *Woodpecker Taps* (p. 3).

Peacock Strut

(for R.H. alone)

Lively

1 *on* __?   *Play close to the keys!*

mf

Repeat playing
1 octave HIGHER.

5

Ostrich Walk

(for L.H. alone)

Lively

mf **1** *on*   ?

Repeat playing
1 octave LOWER.

5

- Can you pat your head and rub your stomach at the same time?
  It is tricky because you are doing two different motions at the same time.

  In this exercise, the L.H. **holds a note down** while the R.H. plays **staccato**.

R.H. Warm-Up

- Play these fingers together
  several times on the piano lid.

Keyboard Trick!

Moderately fast

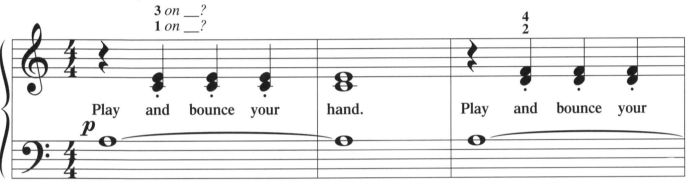

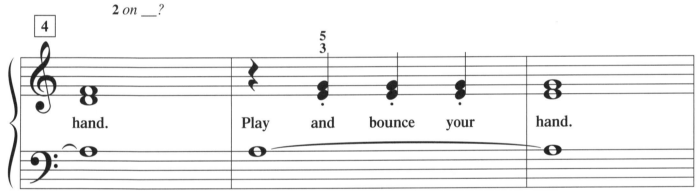

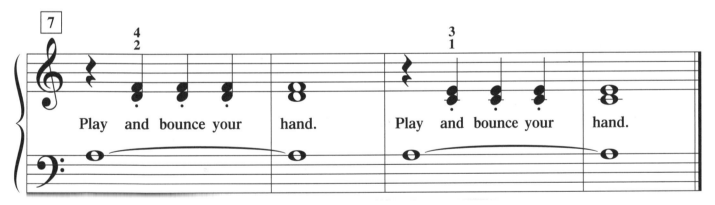

 Can you play this piece with the R.H. 1 octave *higher!*

Teacher Duet: (Student plays *1 octave higher*)

Lesson p.15 (The Haunted Mouse)

Artistry means playing the music with expression or feeling.

- Listen to your teacher play *The Wild Colt*. Does the music create a mood or **"sound picture"**?

- Can YOU create a "sound picture" as you practice *The Wild Colt*?

  1. Could the *staccato* sounds be horse hooves running quickly?
  2. For the *legato* section, can you picture the wild colt running up and down the hills?
  3. At the end of the piece, could the colt be disappearing into the moonlight?

The Wild Colt

Rather quickly

N. Faber

Teacher Duet: (Student plays *1 octave higher*)

🎹 Lesson p.17 (Young Hunter)   FF1C

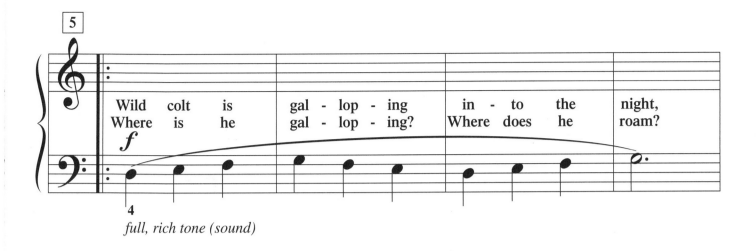

full, rich tone (sound)

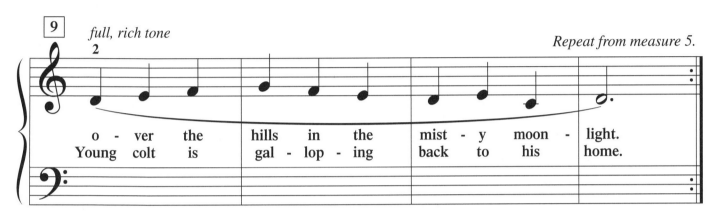

Repeat from measure 5.

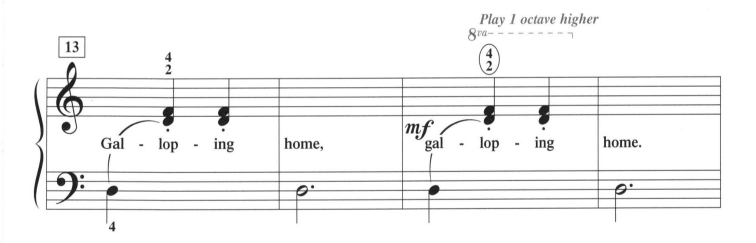

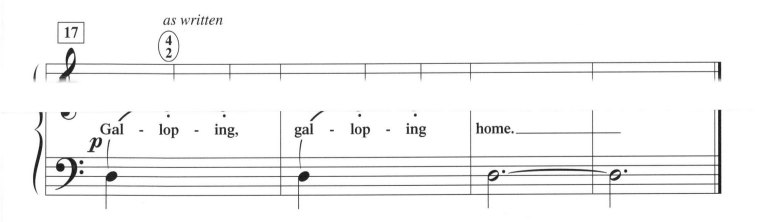

Technique Secret:
round hand shape

Warm-up with *Hand Cups* (p. 2).

- Imagine each **staccato note** is a popcorn seed. Pop the popcorn with a crisp, staccato sound!

- Before playing, circle **step** or **skip**.

Pop! Pop! Popcorn!

Words by Crystal Bowman

Bouncing happily

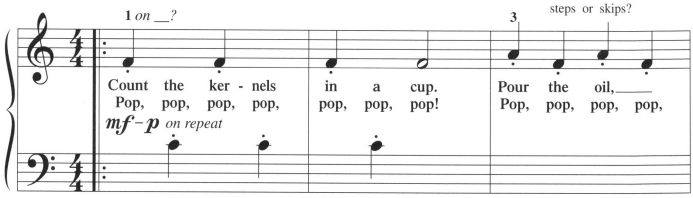

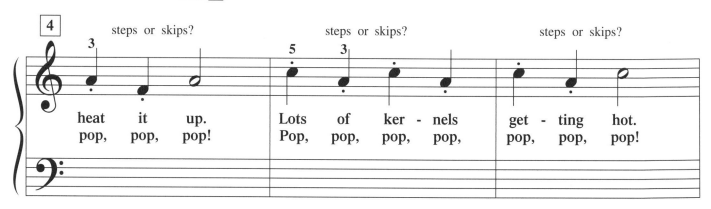

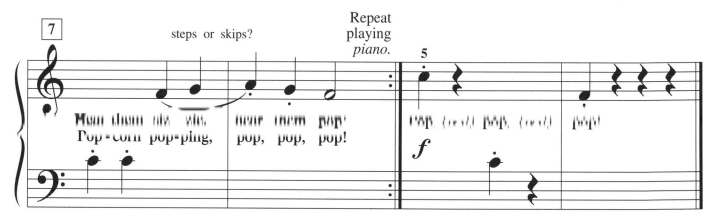

Lesson p.18 (Skipping in Space)

- Review: Demonstrate a "wrist float-off" for your teacher before playing.

- Imagine your right hand as a rising balloon. Let your wrist gently rise on the "air currents."

Hold the damper pedal down throughout.

Floating Balloon

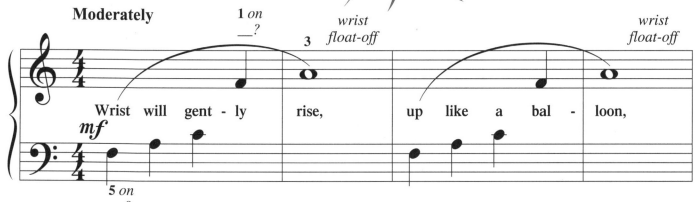

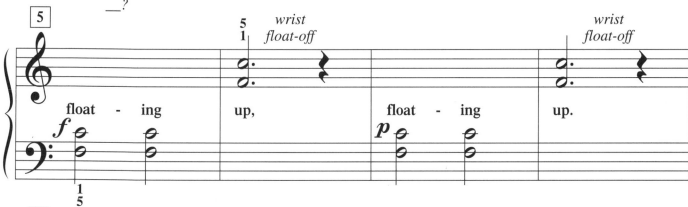

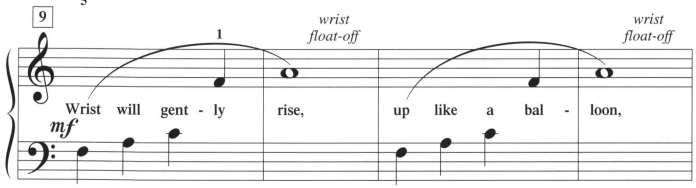

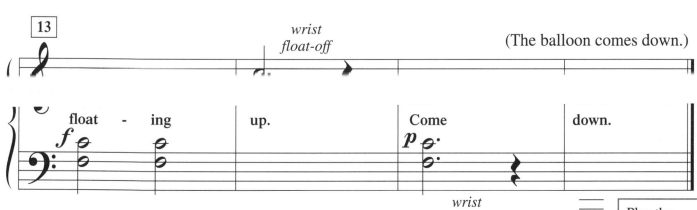

(The balloon comes down.)

Play the LOWEST F on the piano.

Lesson p.20 (The Lonely Pine)

Technique Secret:
finger independence

Do *Finger Talk* (R.H., L.H., then H.T.) using this pattern:

5 - 4 - 3 - 2 - 1 - 2 - 3 - 4 - 5

A pianist with good technique **PREPARES** the next hand position.

• Move one hand to the next position while the other hand is still playing.

Tree House

Walking swiftly

1 on
—?

McArthur

mf

(L.H. begins crossing over.)

5 on
—?

5

(R.H. prepares.)

8va – (1 octave higher)

R.H.

5

L.H.

9

(8va)

(R.H. begins crossing over.)

L.H.

13

(L.H. prepares.)

Lesson p.24 (Paper Airplane)

FF1

In this piece, a secret is told in the last line of music.

- Play the music at the very end of the piece softly.
  The secret is being whispered!

Roses Are Red

N. Faber

Happily

mp Ros - es are red, vio - lets are blue.

5 *on*
___?

mf Here is a se - cret that's just for you.

Ros - es are red, vio - lets are blue.
mp
(prepare) ①

Play softly, like a whisper.

mf I like pi - an - o and *p* I like you!
wrist float-off

Teacher Duet: (Student plays *1 octave higher*)

097

 Technique Secret:
light hand bounce

- Write your own rhythm in $\frac{4}{4}$ using staccatos. ✏

- Do *Woodpecker Taps* (p. 3) using your rhythm.

$\frac{4}{4}$ | ‖

- Before playing, name the intervals
(**2nd** or **3rd**) in each blank. ✏

Mouse on a Trampoline
C 5-Finger Scale

Rather quickly

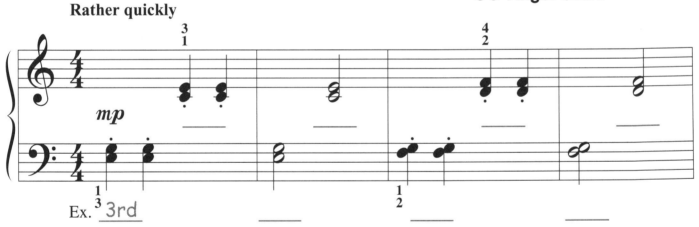

mp

Ex. **3rd**

rest! *f*

 SUPER STUDENT Play the right hand one octave *higher.*

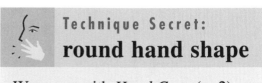

Technique Secret:
round hand shape

Warm-up with *Hand Cups* (p. 2).

This 1 is 4 You
(for R.H. alone)

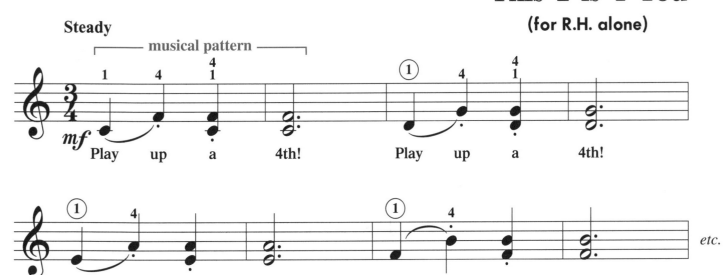

Continue this pattern beginning on G, A, B, and C.

This 1 is 4 You, 2!
(for L.H. alone)

Continue this pattern beginning on F, E, D, and C.

Play each exercise again using **fingers 2** and **5**.

Lesson p.30 (A Mixed-Up Song)

Technique Secret:
finger independence

Do *Finger Talk* (R.H., L.H., then H.T.) using this pattern:

1 - 4 - 3 - 2 - 5 <u>hold</u>

- Circle all the **4ths** in this piece.

Moderately fast

Racing Bikes

mf Rac- ing down the | cit - y streets, the | bik - ers round the | curve.

5

Up and down the | hills, they pass each | oth - er with a | swerve.

9

Ev - 'ry - bod - y's | cheer - ing as they | near the fin - ish | line.

13

"Num-ber Four" is | lead - ing now, and | wins in rec - ord | time!

The last bike to finish had a flat tire. Play the piece again slowly and *staccato*.

Technique Secret:

relaxed wrist

Warm-up with *Wrist Float-off* (p. 2).

Magic Doorbells

Slowly and gracefully

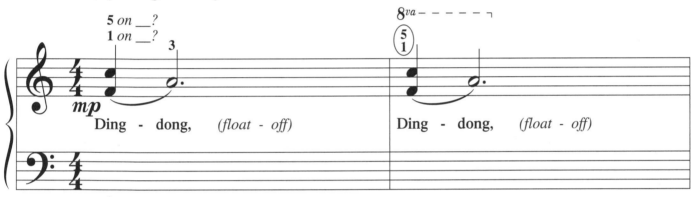

5 *on* __?
1 *on* __?   3

Ding - dong,   *(float - off)*

8*va* - - - - - ⌐
⑤
①

Ding - dong,   *(float - off)*

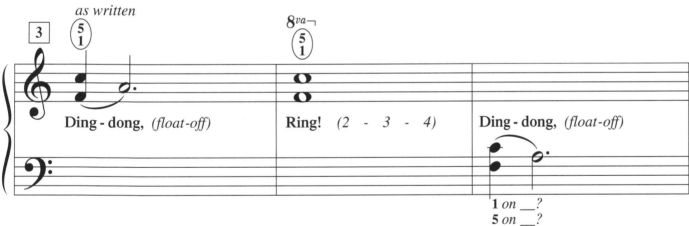

3   ⑤ *as written*
①

Ding - dong, *(float-off)*

8*va*⌐
⑤
①

Ring!   *(2 - 3 - 4)*

Ding - dong, *(float-off)*

1 *on* __?
5 *on* __?

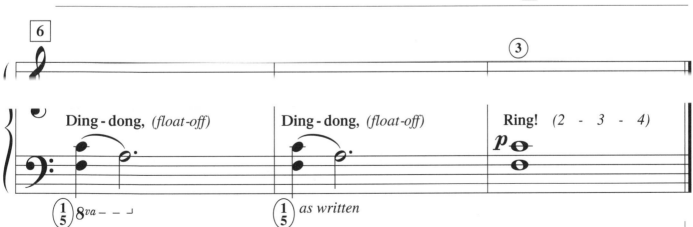

6

③

Ding - dong, *(float-off)*

Ding - dong, *(float-off)*

Ring!   *(2 - 3 - 4)*
p

①   8*va* - - ⌐
⑤

① *as written*
⑤

Lesson p.34 (Rain Forest)   19

Different **DYNAMICS** (*p, mp, mf, f*) help to make a piece interesting.

In this piece, **you can choose the dynamics**.

- First, read the words and play the music.
- Then write dynamic marks in the boxes given.
- Now play with your own last line of lyric.

Legend* of the Buffalo

With spirit

N. Faber

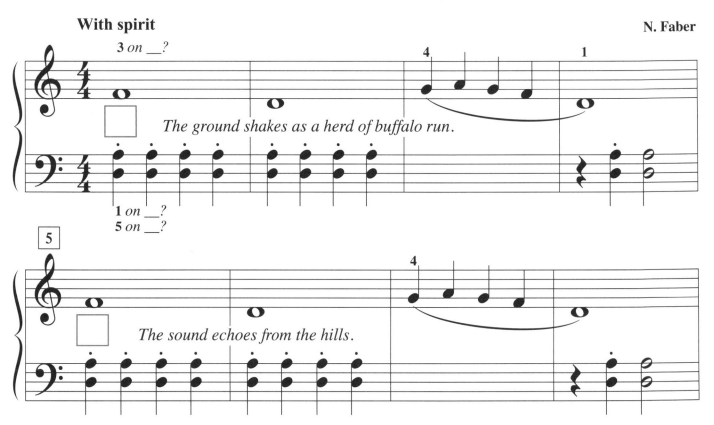

3 on __?

The ground shakes as a herd of buffalo run.

1 on __?
5 on __?

The sound echoes from the hills.

Teacher Duet: (Student plays *as written*) Note: Follow the dynamic marks chosen by the student.

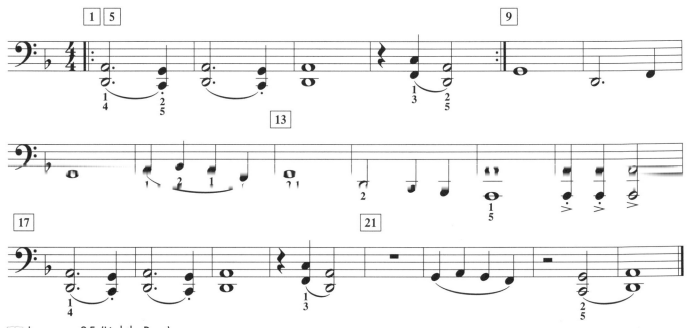

The deer and wolves stop and listen.

gradually play louder

The largest buffalo is over 2500 pounds!

A dust cloud rises as the mighty buffalo thunder by.

(You write the last sentence.)

(omit 8va
for duet)

*There are many Native American legends that honor and respect the mighty buffalo.

Technique Secret:
finger independence

Do *Finger Talk* (R.H., L.H., then H.T.) using this pattern:
5 - 3 - 5 - 3 - 4 - 2 - 4

• First play on the closed piano lid.
  Hint: Both hands use the **same fingering**.

Busy Machine

Blind Flying — to play by memory, looking **straight ahead**, NOT at your hands.

• Memorize the musical pattern for *Bat Sonar*, then play it "blind flying."

Bat Sonar
(for R.H. alone)

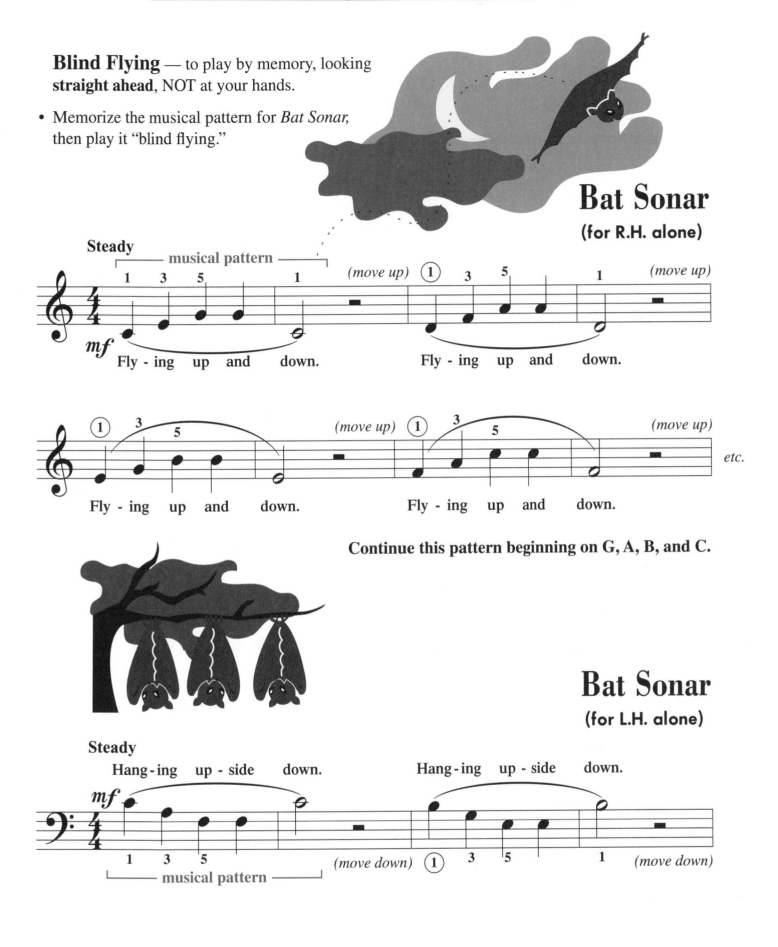

Continue this pattern beginning on G, A, B, and C.

Bat Sonar
(for L.H. alone)

Continue this pattern beginning on F, E, D, and C.

Lesson p.38 (No Moon Tonight)

Have you ever looked through a kaleidoscope?
You would see many beautiful colors.

In music, playing the **dynamics** creates "musical colors."

- Create "musical colors" in this piece by following the dynamics closely.

- Before playing, name the **intervals** (2nd, 3rd, 4th, or 5th) in the blanks. ✏

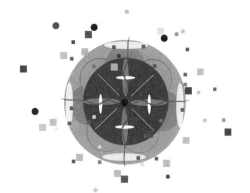

Kaleidoscope Colors

Hold the damper pedal down throughout.

N. Faber

Rather slowly

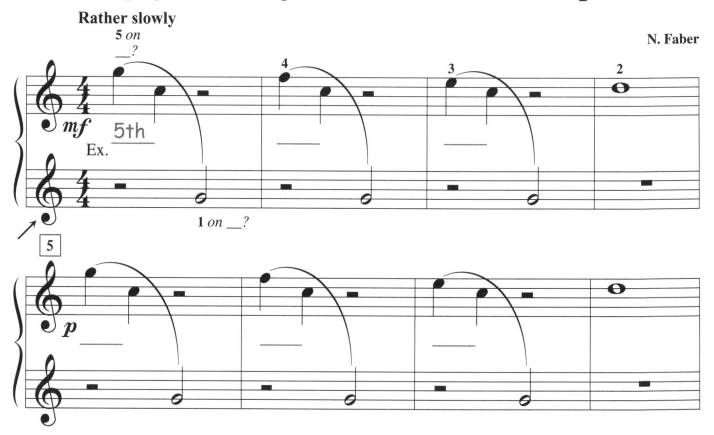

Teacher Duet: (Student plays *as written*) Teacher pedals for duet.

📖 Lesson p.39 (Grumpy Old Troll)   FF1(

- Use your imagination and choose a color for each dynamic mark.

  p _____   *mp* _____   *mf* _____   *f* _____

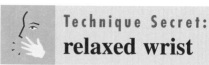

Technique Secret:
relaxed wrist

Warm-up with *Wrist Float-off* (p. 2).

- When playing from a **white key** to a **black key**, let your hand roll forward (toward the piano).

- As your fingers "walk up" to the black key, your wrist will rise *slightly*.

Play
L.H.

walk up

Play
R.H.

walk up

Waves Rolling In

Rather slowly

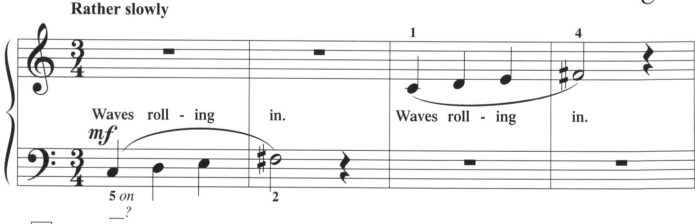

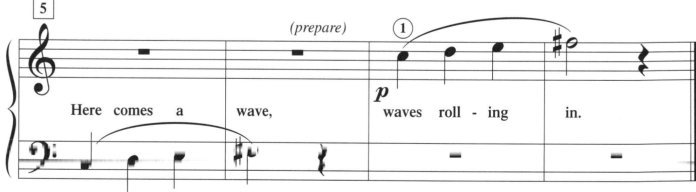

Repeat playing the quarter notes *staccato*.
Your wrist should rise, just as when playing *legato*.

To play with artistry, a pianist must **LISTEN**.

- In this piece, can you continue to hear the right hand **"meow"** while the left hand plays?

Tomcat Howl

McArthur, Faber, Faber

Mysteriously

3 *on* Eb
2 *on* D

f MEOW!   Tom - cat   prowl - ing,

p

5 *on* __?   3   1

[4]

walk - ing   up   the   al - ley - way.   Tom - cat

5   1   2   ⑤   3
move!   8*va* – – – – – –

[7]

howl - ing.   This   is   what   he   has   to   say:

1   (8*va*) – – – – – – –

[10]   3
       2   *Listen to the sound!*   ⌢ hold
       1

f

Don't lift until the sound

Play the
LOWEST C
on the piano!

You and your teacher may wish to time how long (in seconds) the *howl* at measure 10 lasts until it has completely faded away.

_____ *seconds*

③

📖 Lesson p.44 (Boogie on Broadway)

Technique Secret:
round hand shape

Warm-up with *Hand Cups* (p. 2).

This piece uses only **tonic** and **dominant** notes.

• Hint: Begin crossing the *left hand over* while the right hand is still playing.

Gymnastics

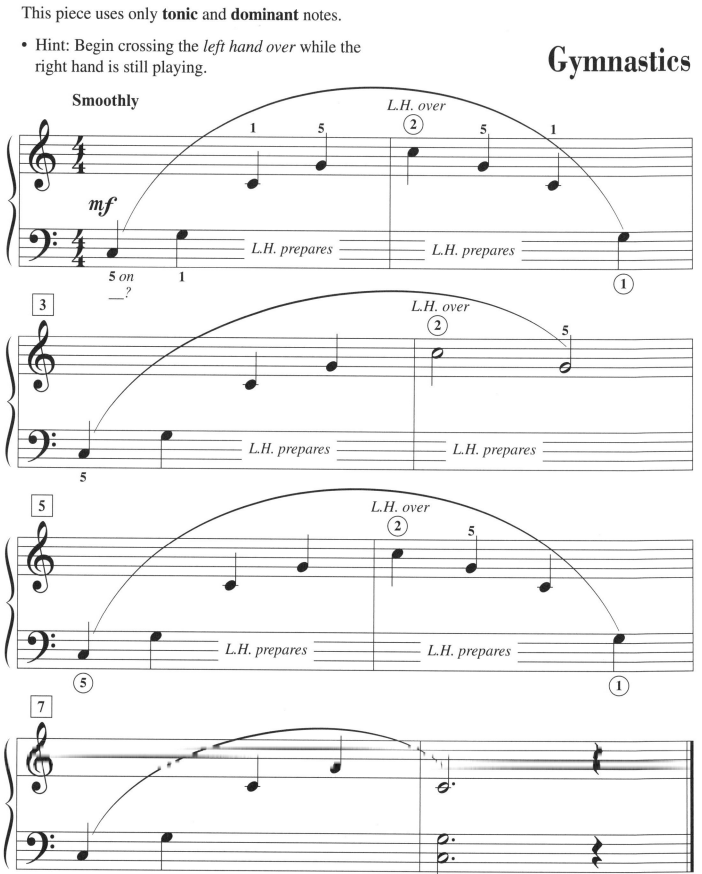

This piece combines many of the musical ideas
you have learned:

1. steady rhythm
2. legato and staccato
3. dynamics
4. listening

• Does your performance include them all?

Camel's Journey

Music by N. Faber

Play the right hand one octave *higher*.

Lesson p.47 (Girl/Boy on a Bicycle)   29

Technique Secret:
round hand shape

Warm-up with *Hand Cups* (p. 2).

Rock Climbing

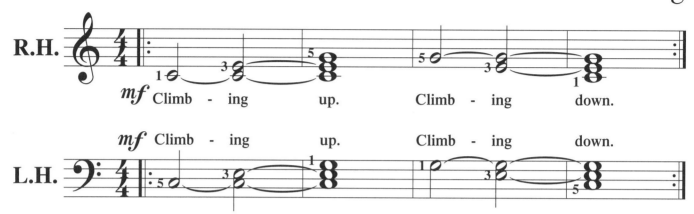

R.H.
mf Climb - ing up. Climb - ing down.

mf Climb - ing up. Climb - ing down.
L.H.

- For *forte* chords, play to the bottom of the keys with a relaxed wrist.

- For *piano* chords, play lightly and close to the keys.

Chord Cakewalk*

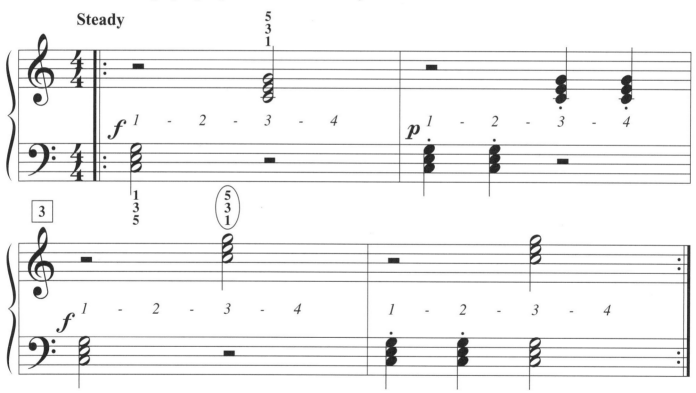

Steady

f 1 - 2 - 3 - 4 *p* 1 - 2 - 3 - 4

f 1 - 2 - 3 - 4 1 - 2 - 3 - 4

*A cakewalk is a march-like dance with prancing high steps. A cake was the prize for the best dancers.

Teacher Duet: (Student plays *1 octave higher*)

R.H.

L.H. *mf* *p* *mf*

An **artistic ending** puts the finishing touch on a piece.

For the last line of this piece:

- Practice s-l-o-w-i-n-g down and getting softer.
- Do a wrist float-off on the last note.
- Lift the pedal and place both hands in your lap.

Hold the damper pedal down throughout.

Carousel

N. Faber

- Did you play an artistic ending?
  Listen to your teacher applaud!

Lesson p.51 (Row, Row, Row Your Boat)   31

V⁷

Technique Secret:
light hand bounce

Do *Woodpecker Taps* (R.H., L.H., then H.T.)

Use this rhythm: ¾ ♩ ♩ ♩ | ♩ 𝄾 𝄾 :‖

Rhythm Hint

- Drop into **beat 1** of each measure.

- Play beats 2 and 3 lightly, staying close to the keys.

Baseball Game

Play 3 times
(or you're out!)

Light and happy

Teacher Duet: (Student plays *as written*. Teacher plays both hands *1 octave higher* throughout.)

Melody: the tune

Harmony: notes or chords played with the melody

Hint: Make the harmony softer than the melody.

Trading Baseball Cards

McArthur, Faber, Faber

Lesson p.54 (Shepherd's Song)   33

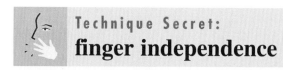

Technique Secret:
finger independence

Do *Finger Talk* (R.H., L.H., then H.T.) using this pattern:

5 - 3 - 1 - 3 - 1 - 3 - 5

This exercise uses 4 different **G 5-finger scales**.

- Prepare each new G scale during the half rest.
- Before playing, find and circle the *ritard*.

Hiking on a New Path

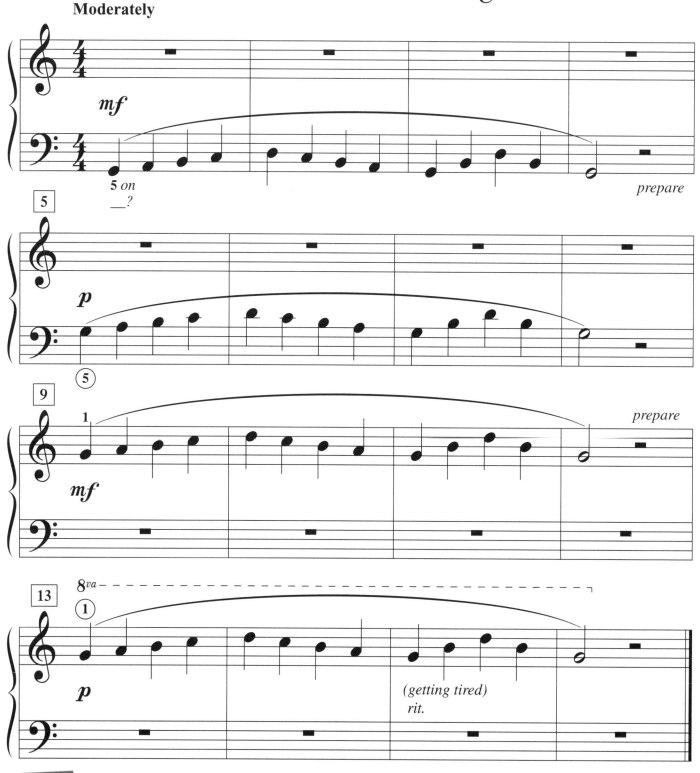

Moderately

mf

5 on
___?

prepare

5

p

⑤

9

1

mf

prepare

13

8*va* ─ ─ ─ ─ ─

①

p

(getting tired)
rit.

Repeat playing *staccato* and *mp* as you hike on a rocky path.

Technique Secret:
light hand bounce

Do *Woodpecker Taps* (R.H., L.H., then H.T.)

Use this rhythm:

- Before playing, name each **interval** in the blanks (2nd, 3rd, 4th, 5th).

Sidewalk Game

Playfully

mf Ex. 2nd

5

9

Hint: Both hands use the same fingering.

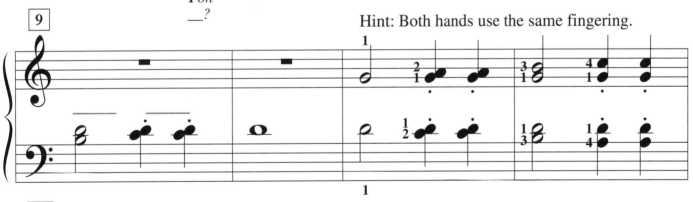

13

Can you memorize and play this piece "blind flying"? (See page 23 for review.)

Can you memorize and play this piece "blind flying"? (See page 23 for review.)

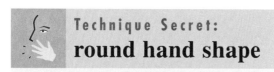

Technique Secret:
round hand shape

Warm-up with *Hand Cups* (p. 2).

Accent Warm-Up

- Tap this exciting rhythm with your teacher. Count aloud.

- Tap **heavily** for each accent. Tap *lightly* for the other beats.

Prehistoric Rock

1 *on* __?
5 *on* __?

5 *on* __?
1 *on* __?

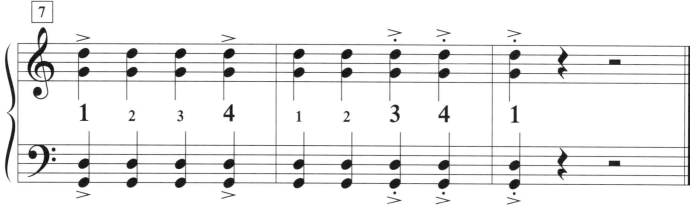

Teacher Duet: (Student plays *as written*)

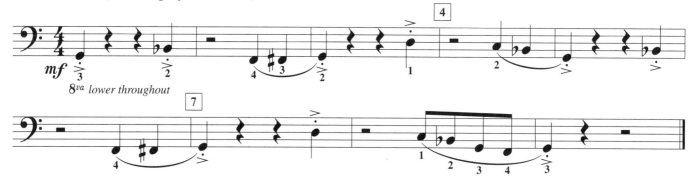

8va lower throughout

🔖 Lesson p.58 (Dinosaur Stomp)

FF10

The Upbeat

An **upbeat** leads into the first beat of the next measure.
The first beat of the measure is called the **downbeat**.

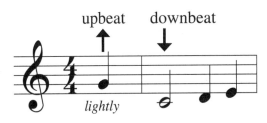

lightly

Upbeat Rule: Play the upbeat *lightly*,
then play a stronger tone on the downbeat.

Before playing the melodies below:

- draw an **up-arrow** over each upbeat.
- draw a **down-arrow** over each downbeat.

Home on the Range

Ex.
mf
Oh, give me a home

Good Morning to You

mf Good morn - ing to you

The Muffin Man

mp Oh, do you know the muf-fin man

Billy Boy
(This melody has 2 upbeats)

mf Oh,— where have you been

When the Saints Go Marching In
(This melody has 3 upbeats)

mf Oh, when the saints go march-ing in,

Point out a melody that begins on **beat 2**, on **beat 3**, on **beat 4**.

🔖 Lesson p.59 (The Dreydl Song)

With your teacher, look through this piece to find the following:

1. slurs
2. staccatos
3. dynamic marks
4. accent marks

Show your artistry in this final piece!

Ocean, Ocean

Music by N. Faber
Words by Crystal Bowman

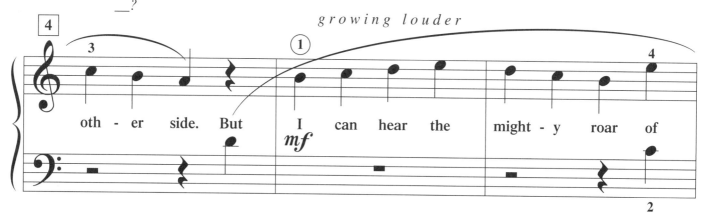

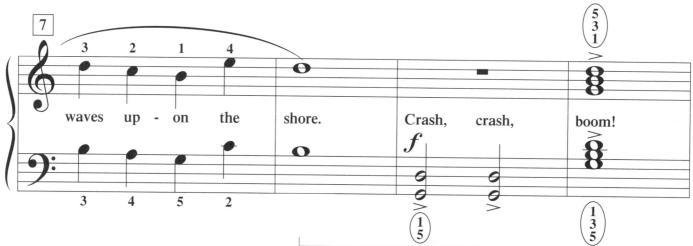

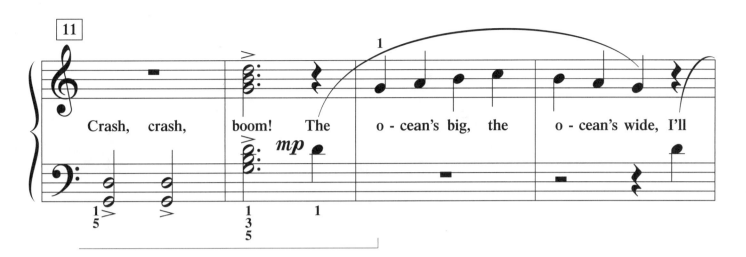

Crash, crash, boom! The o - cean's big, the o - cean's wide, I'll

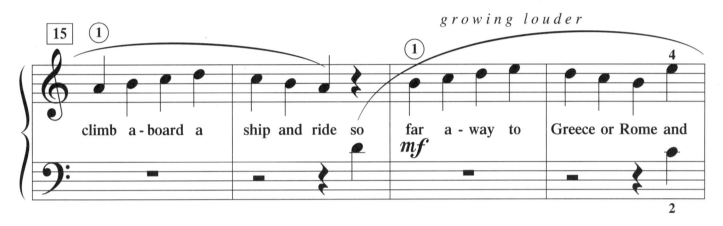

growing louder

climb a - board a ship and ride so far a - way to Greece or Rome and

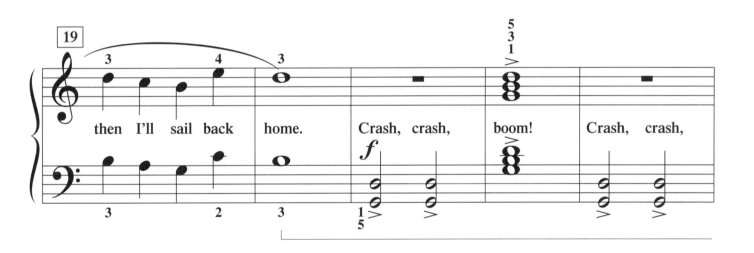

then I'll sail back home. Crash, crash, boom! Crash, crash,

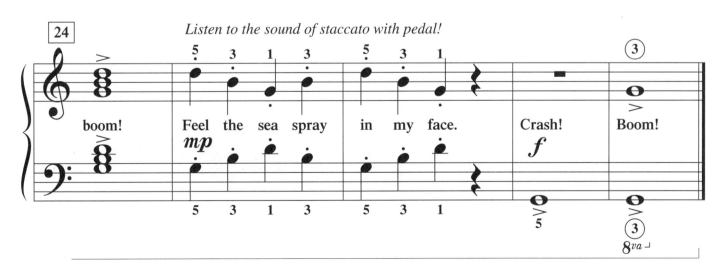

Listen to the sound of staccato with pedal!

boom! Feel the sea spray in my face. Crash! Boom!

Certificate of Fabulous Fingers

Congratulations to:

_____

(Your Name)

You have completed LEVEL 1 TECHNIQUE & ARTISTRY

and are now ready for LEVEL 2A

Teacher:_____

Date:_____